In Memory of Gyles

For Susan, Louise and David

INDEX

Arundel	1
Laugharne	2
St James' Park	4
Woodbury Hill	5
Evening Walk (1)	6
Evening Walk (2)	8
Cuckoo	9
Storm	10
Sun-Shadow	11
Time	12
Neighbours	14
Snowfall	15
Father and Son	16
Compline	17
Long Stay	18
Requiem	19
For Catherine	20
Evening Train	21
Meditations on a Chateau	22
At the RA	24
Keep in Touch	25
Hospital Ward	26
For JBW at Newdigate	28
Skies	29

Threshold	30
Snapshot	31
Fragments	32
Once	33
Southern Region	34
Meeting	36
Presence	37
The Widow	38
London	39
Geriatric	40
Crematorium	41
Seasons	42
School Train	43
Snow	44
Protest	45
A Garden	46

Arundel

One day far off this moment
will be long ago, filed awkwardly
in time, its details blurred
by memory's tricks, embellishments
and change. It will be so important
to be right, to know within the space
between us how you looked
and spoke and stood. Will you think
you took my hand and smiled?
And will I know you turned
and left me wanting one sealed moment
of your time? Will there be other witness
to this day? Will they recall the heat,
the sudden cool on grass like paint
beneath the trees – and if the flowers
were white? Only I will know the way
my dress felt on my arms, a sense
which I can summon still, as strong
and soft as in that chill of parting.
Thoughts of you in age are far away
as summer thoughts of snow –
instead I'll hold to us upon that day,
forever poised, untried
by future's cruelties and rewards,
with you forever miraged,
waiting and unchanged,
soul shadow wordless in my heart.

Laugharne

Tucked like a secret pride outside the town
close by the rain-hued sea,
I find this haven of your mind,
this chapel to your art.

All here is faint, unsung –
an artist's sketch for morning,
its stillness homage
to your dear presence gone.

A cool path leads me on
to this small hut
set casually against the bay,
its walls now bramble-hung –

its door inset with glass.
Hands cupped, I peer inside
to see your table, chair –
another broken one,

scrawled writings, papers
thrown, a bottle,
Woodbine pack, a pen:
a haunting now contrived

yet vivid with the sense
that you might soon return,
had stopped outside awhile
to feel the sea-cooled air,

to catch anew the fingerings
of thought on drifting days
you found. Here where
you dreamt and dreamed

is sadness held and definition
stirred. Here where you wove your truth
and sang – dark pilgrim casting
defiant prayers upon a blue black sea.

St James' Park

Here you may not find
the private peace
and restoration you had planned.
It isn't here,
not with the people
milling with the birds –
feeding each other's needs.

Nor can you be still at heart
as you had planned,
let go restraint,
solve corners of your life.

You can but forge unspoken empathy
with lovers and the wandering old,
snatch at something lost
that you and they perhaps have never found –
the cradle image of a child
once loved, once also lost.

Spent fantasies emblazoned
on the benches and the grass
are refracted
by the vagrant fettered freedom
of this marvellous park.

Don't get me wrong –
it's a lovely place in which to stroll
to mourn
to dream belief –
and silently to sing one's needs
beneath the sky's bright prayer.

Woodbury Hill

As we walked and climbed
your words rolled back at me like stones,
their harsh truth
cold as hail against my face.
My stumbling steps were frail as my response –
frail as the balance in my thoughts:
my strength was weak that day,
weak as the sun's pale light
reflected in the sea's cool distance
groping for its blue idiom of power.
All was bland that day
except your words of stone.
And blandly too along the shore
a loving couple hand-in-hand
mirrored our easy past –
before the gifts of cruelty marred our ways.

Evening Walk (1)

The gate clicks shut behind me
and like entering a photograph
I part the stillness of the fields –
sure in my offering of time
their waiting welcome to return.
Instead I find beneath the burden
of the sun's demands
the day has held its pose too long,
its mouth is dry –
it shimmers in retreat,
sapped now, as though in age, of all rapport.

Wheat rustles at my side,
nodding me past.
Cows beg for my intrusion,
knowing my fear of their soft power.

An alien now, I climb the stony path
of grass and pungent flower,
as birds sharpen and rehearse
their morning song.

A small church crouches by the road
hinting at benediction.
I enter its cool asylum –
its history host to mystery and faith.
Within its emptiness I pick up
hints of solace, clues
in the eternal treasure-hunt for peace.
I vow myself a promise to return,
but as I pray uncertainly for God
belief slides out of focus,
full commitment fades,
fearing the water's depth.
Am I not safer on the edge?

Evening Walk (2)

Outside the heat nags on,
bewildering the trees who beg
compassion for an innocence of crime,
and in defence can offer only shade.

I turn onto the asphalt track,
my quiet shoes' tread unheard.
A haunting smell of tar entangling
the present with the past,

dusting with memory
the hedge and wandering rose.
A car hums past with common sense –
urging me from dreams.

As though re-grouping from attack,
houses and gates are shut and strange,
compounding solitude –
destroying something I had nearly found.

Cuckoo

Somewhere on the edge of day
a cuckoo plucks the sky,
cool-wooded, far
away it calls
rogue-high above
the faithful chimes of dawn.
Faint, haunting, nearer
now then far,
awake, awake, it calls,
and somewhere
on the edge of thought
a memory starts.
The fraud who simply hopes
his presence may redeem his faults
sings hard to catch the past,
to charm those wintered dreams anew.
The prodigal unfairly lifts the heart.

Storm

Lashed by a feral wind,
the winter sea dons caps of snow
and rides to take its vengeance on the shore –
a cowering victim who has borne it all before;
like powerless love, again it takes the rap.
Frenziedly the trees respond,
encouraged in their own caprice,
their stricken arms now parted
to reveal a shaky moon,
shimmering like a torch
held by an infirm hand.

Later, gently sponged of cloud,
a mellow sky, the laureate of power and light,
calls *pax* for night,
leaving the cool ache of the waves
in respite from their ceaseless repertoire,
to duck and weave
towards the stone-faced gossip town,
where rain by now has also had its say.
The gauntlet of its fury,
thrown on road and field, puddles
to lie unchallenged and ashamed.

Sun-Shadow

Sun swoops to lick
the shadows from the ground.
It pulses clouds to race the wind.
It gleams and darts
along a spoon-smoothed sea.
It rushes rocks,

and sparkles waves
which claw the shore
and fall and rise
in helpless strength,
like children tired beyond their rest.
It blindly floods the hills,

and, as in dreams,
too fast, beyond control,
across the valleys
drowned, it dives –
soared like a floating, silent bird –
gone in a wink-shut eye.

Time

Once more a year is spent,
our numbered days are calendered away –
the writing's on the wall.
Somehow time is passed,
the diary filled,
the pages turned,
arrangements now struck through.

We count the hours,
we claim the days –
with carefully repetitioned acts
we store the sad precision of our lives.

Clocks pound at silence
in the empty house.
Time against time –
night into day –
a sombre slide from dark to light
measures the steady drip of age.

All life is limbo,
moment to moment –
stones
lifting and falling.

As pace keeps pace
and years fall into years
the wheel is turned –
tomorrow's time is here.
As love withholds loving
so living fades,
and death, the shadow-footstepped one,
demands its place.

Chance made too late and lost,
the heart's regret unlearned,
the petal falls –
the pale rose fractures into scent
as night is pressed
by darkness into day.

Neighbours

Full summer voices my neighbour's day –
its echoes ring in mine.
Her radio against the taut blue sky
invades my mind.
Her garden baked at noon
upholds the strangeness of this hour.
Her washing staged
hangs cardboard-still
within the breathless air.
Thin murmurings and laughter
float to a pool of shade –
the open-windowed sounds of home.
These strands are mine
And tell me more than she would have me know.

Snowfall

Snow settles on the scars of winter
blandly like time, healing.
The gaunt trees, soothed
by whitened breath on breath,
deepen in silence
the heart's quiet pain,
till only the bird's thin cry
can pierce this iron land.

A grief untouched,
like water round a stone
though soothed by many tides,
lies still, intact, alone.

Consumed, the open wound may cleanse,
unstaunched by kindness,
breathe within its own renewing fire,
while peace imposed
may purchase truth's sharp pain,
contain the searing heart,
the breath of bone.

Yet this will flood in its own time.
Its constant unheard beat
will storm against the loss
of true loss
lost within compassion's cheer –
will cry against the earth's renewing twin –
against its resurrecting winds and rain,
its sun's sweet flow –
blandly like time.

Father and Son

The boy watches his father
step lightly from his past,
like shedding a towel
or a dead skin,
and turn to his new love
as easily as a fish turns in the sea.

Beneath the clear blue statement of the sky
the sea lies still and guiltless
on good perspective
from the far horizon's line.
High above a bi-plane putters
like a sound-effect
while children play
at timeless untaught games.

The boy watches
at this ordered calm,
relentless as the certainty
of music's limpid notes
from some more structured age.

Already a snapshot in his father's dream,
the boy sees him run and laugh
wearing gauche ill-fitting borrowed youth.
Helpless and unhelped, he watches, stares –
his bold face geared to happiness
he calls out –
but not for an answer.

Compline

In granite cold
the harsh serge voices
meld to the church's stone.

True note for note,
like limpid drops of water
or the unseen petal's fall,
they build a gradual whole.

As the doubter
will repeatedly declaim
to hide his fears,
so they rechant their faith,
in daily need perhaps
to strengthen its belief –

a vaulted cry,
a plea to prove
that wisdom rules
their strangled, saintly lives.

Long Stay

The old lie flat,
washed up on the wrong shore –
their eyes closed
against the cruel mistake
which brought them here –
or wakeful, they watch
as nervously as birds
each move or glance
which might point
ways for their escape.

Their wisdom deep and long-contained,
if now collectively released,
could staunch and overturn
the antiseptic flow of institutional care.
But here it finds no voice –
its faith and patience
smothered in the job-lot
understanding of the old.

Thus do the meek conform,
lie low at levels lost to those who rule.
Like prisoners working for parole
they hide all strength
and silently await their chance –
returning smile for smile
within a dark incontinence of grief.

Requiem

Sorrow breaks like winter in the night –
long days of punishment and loss
enforce the burden of recall
with hope receding like a tide.

Words, too, retreat,
tread water in the mind
where memory stores
the gentle core of love,
the comfort of the unexpressed.

Long years have gone,
and still the calm, demanding days
can parable the past.

The cruel sweet sun
can sharpen still the heart,
probing its pain,
its poignant warmth
as hollow as mistaken cheering.
Trespassing on the past
I haunt our precious ways.

I wait in prayer
while on and on
despair's adrenaline
sustains the strength
of this my requiem for you,
wounding that pain
whose wise simplicity,
beyond the need for words,
telepathically enforces and upholds
the long enquiry of the soul.

For Catherine

From birth to birth
is birth reborn
and life retold –
the circle joined,
the child a mother's made.

Safe-sheltered now
in solemn care,
still centre of our joy,
a talisman towards our own rebirth,
the common-place made rare.

Dark shreds of memory stir –
we search you for
a meaning we can tap –
a truth so slender, fine,
it should be wrapped impossibly
and held, like water
cupped within the hand
against time's thefting change.

Evening Train

dog rose and daisy
cinder track –
child voices
feathered breeze
warm evening sun
on asphalt paths
a door slams
someone's going home
soft field's reflection
in river's limpid light
stone pictures thrown
against the mind
late children's games
a woman in her window, stilled
a man alone
what chance has held them
in this frame
unknown, not knowing me yet
ever to haunt, profound they stay
a faint intensity
uninvented in my mind
a whisper of some truth
a poem I cannot find

Meditations on a Chateau

1.
Serene among your ghosts,
you stand aloof to wraiths which haunt
you now and prey like fleas
upon a beast too proud to stir.

2.
Great-eyed beyond the gravelled walk you stare,
alert above the scrabble of today
for sounds no longer heard,
for carriages and splendours lost –
mourning with a loyalty
which increases with despair.

3.
Through cool dead rooms
where shivered history blows
our blind stares meet,
dark portraits long-resigned
to share a stranger's eye
follow the raw crowd's roam.

4.
Across the day-leaved floors,
roped now from rooms
where life once played,
your splendours are intoned –
posed now but still assured
as beauty which is proved
and needs no balm.

5.
Bereaved, the careful gardens wait,
groomed with a ritual expertise
yet free in the strange ways of space.
With grace the flowers take their turn –
wallflowers and roses bow to roses' scent,
and dappled lawns lie cool
beneath paternal shade.

6.
The deep-treed lake
reflects its memorial past
and sees us not,
perhaps with age
now stored too full
to hold the shadows of today.

7.
Pared down to history's bone,
we share with you shared past,
more vivid in this emptied world
than in houses filled with families
who claim a private heritage
and tread alone
the paths of their lost shores.

At The RA
– Treasures from Ancient Nigeria, a legacy of 2000 years

This morning we have seen the past
in images which block today.
Distanced by a measure more than time,
these ancient forms so carefully displayed
speak of a wisdom lost,
a truth long buried
where once such heads had lain.

Of what then do they tell,
these Kings and Queens and humbler souls
now deified in terracotta, bronze and stone?
Where did they learn
this certainty that each one holds?

Strangely one does not sense
a sculptor's hand –
response is to a living form
as though these numb shapes,
could they speak,
could reach us yet,
could tell of mystery and truth
long locked and lost to man –
mute cries within the stone.

Keep In Touch

all the best
mind how you go
take care
and keep in touch
you have your mobile
I have mine
we're all in touch today
all in the grasp
of net and web
fingering with fear
the fringes of success –
we're double glazed
against the bleak cries
of the orphan
we are not fools
we don't go out at night
forget the stars
and moonlight on the sea
what more can we do?
all's well as long
as we're in touch
good pictures too
when darkness comes
of distant wars
without the stench of blood
of instant gardens
without pests or scents
shown before a picture
of exotic food
our lights stay on
we obey a call for help
we pledge our aid
and painlessly write cheques
or quote our credit cards
perhaps the more we learn
the less we feel
safe in a world
of buy-one-get-one-free
life must go on
so cheer up
mind how you go
take care –
and keep in touch

Hospital Ward

Night looms into morning on the silent ward,
the struggles of the dark are stilled –
as though the actors now are spent
and wait for newer acts to start.
The old are turned, their pains
are soothed with nursery care,
with kindness from the book if not the heart.

A dialogue from the beds begins:
'It's raining still.'
'D'you hear that wind?'
'I haven't slept' –
The chorus grows –
its pattern drowns the day.

A code is fixed,
its mantle falls on all –
a currency is shared
of bantered rules which must be learned
and kept to shape and frame the whole,
as though to keep the play alive.

For here safe levels must be kept,
of temperature and thought,
of bowel and heart.
Visitors and clergy come to soothe,
bearing with gifts and prayer
small pieces of the outer world.

A stand-in may one day arrive,
take, from another suddenly in clothes,
his bed; his part fulfilled,
this one departs to live off-stage,
waved off without farewell,
lost in a thin applause.

Or someone takes the part of Death
and quietly in a whispered corner dies –
a curtained ritual speaks
what none are told –
a door closed on a child –
this is a private realm,
a lapse we must not share.

For JBW at Newdigate

This little church in its nine hundred years
has stood in faith, has surveyed
in change and desecration,
but with a secret strength held fast.
It cannot in its age now
offer more than peace,
can only match our homage
with its hallowed past.

It was here in the end you came,
for we did our best in the end.
No flowers, no letters, no mourning,
you had said. On the last days
when you were not truly here –
dragging yesterday into today
and making it one,
we did our best in the end
but could not quite let go,
resist the last, late spoiling rite –
a prayer, a hymn, a tear
as you were carried from us
to the chilled grass and the stone.

In the end we did our best –
hard to please a departed guest –
chose carefully our thoughts and words,
stepped warily over
the rough edges of your soul –
and lost you sharply,
somewhere in the bland offerings of faith.

Skies

1.
Skulled of colour from
a dream-stilled cry,
the shell sky softens into day.

Against a rook-cold light
the dawn black trees
conspire to brace
and listen for the wind.

2.
In evening's glow
a liquid pool of light
is followed by no colour, pool or light.
As gardeners sense for night
the bright flowers sharpen in the gloom,
their colours darkening in the dark.
In stillness stilled,
a borrowed peace is ours.

Threshold

Sometimes the light stays long,
too long. Just when one yearns
for night, pale evening stays.

Evening is long in light
when blessed dark is due –
when curtains should be drawn
and night begin its secrets.

Either stay, faint fearful light,
or fade, within the bird's sweet evening song.
Don't test me on this shadowed choice.

Snapshot

The baby in his push-chair cries;
his mother with her flat demanding eyes
stares into envy.
He calls louder –
holds out his hand.
Not taken, he snuffles into sleep,
storing later unwept tears –
hoarding rejection.
Like mother, like son.

Fragments

Before we're friends
and after our roles are played,
there's a bridge to cross,
so frail
that neither can take the first step.

***

Love is alone –
I love you yet,
though new to my thoughts
you stay new
to my past and dreams.
You dream
we meet
and in our meeting lose and gain.

***

I am now out of words –
thoughts come
but won't distil:
they float and dream –
no sequence stays.

In this dread state
no fix prevails –
the magnet to the point attracts
but fades –
on contact dies.

Reality too much intrudes.
no gift remains
to still true meaning
in a morning frame.

Once

Once it was children,
now it's plants you tend –
nurturing, feeding,
enjoying the fruits
of nourishment I lend.

And there was that day lately
with you running up the hill
and me following slowly,
seeing in you still
the indelible, vanished shred of childhood.
You turned to watch,
and looked back down the hill,
seeing me perhaps as I too once had been.
You smiled, dreading my age.

Southern Region

The train comes through
misty half-eyed towns
throwing off scrapyards,
corrugated halls and schools,
halting on grass-pathed lines
where houses packed
like crowds along the route
display their careless gardens,
sheds and flowers –
their long-lined cabbages stark, winter-thin.

Through streamered stations
playing-fields and parks
it shreds the air
pounding to match the discipline of time.

Far from disordered peace
and humbler homes
the weedless suburbs start –
seeming to hold their breath
in contemplation of effect,
like carefully tended maidens
who fear their petticoats may show.

Far from the iron heat,
the easy rose,
the tumbling love and hate,
the unthought certainties
that mould and scar
yet wield unspoken strength –
rough justice here seems lost
in symbols of a newer state.

Flash-glimpsed through
ribboned hedge or fence,
late sunlight falls on cattled hills
posed by a god-like hand.
As dusky evening falls
a seperateness descends
between each passenger
beneath his smoky light.
Gone seems the chance
or need to speak –
withdrawal is understood.

A concentration starts,
a careful watching or that
scrutinising other self
who stares in from the dark.

Meeting

I walked up the street
with a woman I had not known.
I am a stranger made.

We talked –
for some reason we talked.
For some lost reason
we needed to talk –
not to each other
but of ourselves.

We are as strangers made.

Yet now I'll wonder
on her life
and she'll ask of me –
though we had not talked
to each other,
but only of ourselves.

Presence

As though before the storm
I see a sharpened sky
black-cut with trees,
tense with the feel of rain.

As though before a dream
I sense a sleep,
a breath withheld.
A wraith of you returned.
As though before the storm
I'm watched in silence on the streets –
the eyes of houses stare –
contained,
like books unread yet filled –
a threatening peace sustained,
to haunt changed paths
and slipping time –
to mourn no second chance.

A waiting game
enclosed –
and echoed in the heart.

The Widow

She walks alone
through fields of time,
pitied and forgotten
like old news.

At night she wakes too soon,
intruding on the privacy of dawn.
Watching the edge of darkness fray,
she searches with lost eyes
for truth or God to form.

As day unfurls
the taunt of spring
yawns in the early light,
teasing her fears –
and yet its hard cold pain and dread
is tempered and assuaged
by something in the air –
the morning hiss of cars,
a weird calm,
the empathy of strangers on their ritual ways.

London

I am at last returned,
returned to the gardens of war,
where the parched sun
had tested earth's survival
all those years ago,
when the famed and brilliant blue
clashed with ribboned white
the high sky's battle lines
so long ago.

I am back in the arms
of fear and joy
of childhood and of love,
a love I did not value then
in all its hidden worth.
Today has lost the impact of those days –
the sun cannot repeat that strength,
the sky its blue.

Geriatric

Seated by the window now
she stares intently at the shadowed day,
where mist in scarves of silence
gathers in the trees –
and slowly into bonfire piles
a man shapes leaves.

The garden view drawn cold
protects her from the view within.
Her face is ill-defined,
its features small,
her pale eyes reflecting unknown loss
her profile says do not disturb.

Safe, dark, the key is turned –
against all worlds the lock is fast.
No one, nothing can reach her now.
She can confound the expert's trials.

Safe, safe, she rocks and smiles,
surrendered, true,
her last self found –
the lost child brought to age.

Crematorium

Beneath October's cruel sun
in dusky afternoon
of bronze and fallen leaves
we come to this dark garden,
here to your resting place.

While the heart hammers
at the dread that you are gone
the gliding cars with fearful timing loom –
smooth-black, as though on rails,
fate sealed, too late for change.

True once for others, now ourselves
a ritual starts,
as murmured words intone,
they hold our pain.
As long as we may mourn and pray
a part of you is here,
the truth is stayed.
Till to a new cold world we file,
strangely,
as though awaiting guidance,
news, for the dream to break.

Sharp flowers are lain,
their colours soft, or crude as paint –
somehow a kindness came too late,
numbed by the aweful peace that holds you now.
We move away
no more to do
we move away.
Gently we move away
and the long days start.

Seasons

Summer lost
is like a love long gone –
and loved
and stronger loved
for its far passing.

Autumn's pride and brilliance
does not bear the strength of spring
whose gentle power
can heal and nourish
as it does the ground –
can shelter growth
and leave the delicate
its own quiet force to flower.

Deep winter in its darkness
veils the heart,
lends time and secret snows
to buy and sustain
the force of truth unsung,
a love not meant to be.

I'm failed and foolish
in my search for identity unmarked,
unproven as are melted footprints
in the snow –
transient as passing cloud or breeze
I'm my own pale ghost,
unwelcome as a stranger in my past.

School Train

The train draws their sons
away into a distance
that is chosen,
small in their suits,
lost in their dormitory years,
these parents wave and weep
for time's lost touch –
the empty house, the hollow heart.

Yet thus they learn
and thus are they prepared, they say,
for future's silent years
when these their sons
will give them tempered love,
pale truths
and strangeness –
flowers on the grave.

Snow

Snow falls and falls,
reluctantly at first
as though its heavy grey-skied bluff
at last were called.

Slowly, stubbornly,
then fast and proud,
released, unlocked, confessing, free
it falls and falls –
seeming to find no end,
as tears once found can reach no end,
as tears can find no end.

Protest

The rain clears suddenly
like something solved,
leaving the air
cold as a clean slate.

Crowds sensibly prepared
and tensed in concord
stand suddenly bereft of cause,
and wrongly dressed –
encumbered with reason
they will not need.

Assurance wanes,
the sun floods back in amnesty,
dissolving theory
and its uniting fears.

A Garden

Your summer comes,
your roses grow,
your garden shines
in some false pose
without you. It holds
the secrets of lost years
and cruelly does not change.

In springtime's stillness too,
or winter's peace
when soft-turned soil lies bare,
in late September's sun
of bronze and scented mists –
in faded days of Michaelmas
in bonfire dusks –
in every season's mood
the chance of you remains
and torn beginnings stir.